MW00803175

THE ESSENTIAL LAST SUPPER

Also by
Ralph E. Jarrells

Jesus * Judas
Fiery Red Hair, Emerald Green Eyes, and a Vicious Irish Temper
Ill Gotten Gain
The Essential Automobile

THE ESSENTIAL LAST SUPPER

RALPH E. JARRELLS

WordCrafts Press

Unless otherwise noted all scripture is taken from the King James Version of the Holy Bible. Public Domain.

ISBN: 978-1-962218-02-3

Cover design by Mike Parker.

Published by WordCrafts Press
Cody, Wyoming 82414
www.wordcrafts.net

To Sybil E. Jarrells.
You are my muse.

Introduction

Research is important to writing novels, especially historic fiction. However, many times you find information that takes you in a different direction. While researching my third novel, *Jesus-Judas: Best Friends Forever*, I found many interesting facts in the Bible that I hadn't seen before or at least didn't remembered. Jesus had seven half brothers and sisters. Matthew 13:55 even gives his half brothers names—James, Joseph Jr., Simon, and Jude (Judas). Harmonizing the four synoptic gospels, I was even able to make a chronology of Jesus preaching/teaching.

In sources other than the Bible, I discovered a lot of information about the Last Supper, some of which was corroborated by the Bible. The Last Supper became the form and format of what Christians sometimes call The Lord's Supper or the Eucharist—one of the sacraments celebrated in Christian churches. It is considered a means of communing with Jesus and as a commemoration of Jesus' death.

The Lord's Supper is one of the essential elements of the Christian religion. But, when someone says, "The Last Supper," the iconic painting by Leonardo da Vinci is likely to come to mind. It has become a part of our *collective consciousness*. Jesus and the Twelve are depicted at this momentous occasion.

Since it was painted 1495–1498, Leonardo was obviously *not* painting from personal knowledge, so it is no surprise that he got it all wrong. Or did he have an ulterior motive? Conspiracy buffs can point to numerous examples of so-called *evidence of esoteric connections* hidden in the picture. Magdalene cults found Mary as one of the disciples. Musical scholars found numerous examples of Pythagorean musical ratios—12:6:4:3. Numerologists say the picture is a playground of numerical references—four groups of three disciples; two groups of four tapestries on the walls separated by three alcoves; three windows in the back wall, and many numerical ties between heaven and earth, the Gospels, and the Trinity. British Broadcasting Company investigative reporters Michael Baigent, Richard Leigh and Henry Lincoln discovered a number of connections between da Vinci and secret cults in their book *Holy Blood, Holy Grail*, a forerunner of Dan Brown's wildly popular international bestselling novel, *The DaVinci Code*. Literally thousands of theologians have attempted to explain the Christian symbolism and truth in the picture and to name the disciples as they sit in the picture.

Regardless of how beloved or revered the painting was and is, apart from its symbolic representation, it was not a true representation of the real Last Supper.

It is essential to remember that Jesus was a practicing Jew and therefore would celebrate all of the Jewish holidays. Also, Jesus was considered a Rabbi , the Hebrew term for *Master*. The Gospels attest that at least twelve times:

- Matthew 26:25—"*Master*, is it I?
- Matthew 26:49—"Hail, *Master*, and kissed him."
- Mark 9:5—"Jesus, *Master*, it is good for us"
- Mark 11:21—"*Master*, behold, the fig tree"
- Mark 14:45—"and saith, *Master*, master"
- John 1:38—"unto him, *Rabbi*, (which is to say, being interpreted, *Master*,) where"
- John 1:49—"Nathanael answered and saith unto him, *Rabbi*, thou art the Son of God"
- John 4:31—"his disciples prayed him, saying, *Master*, eat."

- John 6:25—"they said unto him, *Rabbi*, when camest thou hither?"
- John 9:2—"disciples asked him, saying, *Master*, who did sin "
- John 11:8—"disciples say unto him, *Master*, the Jews of late sought to stone thee"

Even His enemies—Scribes, Pharisees, Sadducees, Herodians—called Him Rabbi at least a dozen times.

- Matthew 9:11—"when the Pharisees saw it, they said unto his disciples, Why eateth your Master with publicans and sinners?"
- Matthew 12:38—"the scribes and of the Pharisees answered, saying, Master, we would see a sign from thee."
- Matthew 17:24—"Doth not your master pay tribute?"
- Matthew 22:16—"the Herodians, saying, Master, we know that thou art true"
- Mark 12:19—"Master, Moses wrote unto us, If a man's brother die"
- Luke 11:45—"Then answered one of the lawyers, and said unto him, Master, thus saying thou reproachest us also."
- Luke 12:13—"said unto him, Master, speak to my brother, that he divide the inheritance with me."
- Luke 19:39—"And some of the Pharisees from among the multitude said unto him, Master, rebuke thy disciples."
- Luke 20:21—"they asked him, saying, Master, we know that thou"
- Luke 20:28—"Saying, Master, Moses wrote unto us"
- Luke 20:39—"Then certain of the scribes answering said, Master, thou hast well said."

Using the King James Version of the Bible, Jewish tradition and historic documentation, this book will attempt to shed some light on the actual Last Supper and provide the means for modern day Christians to celebrate the Last Supper (Seder Meal).

"The noblest pleasure is the joy of understanding."
Leonardo da Vinci

THE PAINTING

The *Last Supper*—*cenacolo* in Italian—by Leonardo da Vinci joins the *Mona Lisa* among the ten most famous paintings in the world according to multiple sources including CNN, *Style,* and Google. It is also one of the most copied and parodied paintings ever created. Commissioned by Ludovico Sforza, the Duke of Milan, it was painted in tempera and oil on a wall in the former Dominican convent Santa Maria della Grazie (Saint Mary of Grace) in Milan, Italy.

Painted 1495 to 1498, it was a notable work for the Italian High Renaissance period. Da Vinci is joined by Michelangelo and Raphael as seminal artist of that time. Large by contemporary standards it is 4.6 by 8.8 meters or about 15 feet by 29 feet.

The Last Supper was never a part of any museum collection partly because of its size, but also because it was a permanent decoration in the convent—it was actually painted on the wall. Originally commissioned as a part of the family mausoleum, when it was finished the room became the refectory, the dining room for the convent.

It has survived wars, restorations, remodeling and the rigors of time. By the early 1500s, the painting had already started to show evidence of deterioration. Initially, the painting's largest enemy was water. The area where the convent is located had an unusually high humidity level. The convent was susceptible to flooding and even steam from the kitchen was a culprit.

A little remodeling caused the first major damage to the painting. In 1652 a door was cut into the north wall removing Jesus' feet and loosening the paint and plaster. Restoration started in 1726, but over the years efforts at restoration actually tended to aggravate the problems they were intended to remedy.

At one point, the refractory was used as a prison. At another

time, Napoleon's troops used the refractory as a stable. Stories of that time suggest that the troops threw rocks at the painting and used it for target practice.

The ravages of modern war also reached the Convent. During World War II, Milan was the most heavily bombed city in Northern Italy. On the night on August 12, 1943, some 478 British bombers targeted Milan. 1,252 tons of bombs were dropped on the region. Santa Maria delle Grazie was in ruins. The roof of the

refractory was partially destroyed and subsequent reconstruction also left the painting open to the elements. It wasn't clear if the bomb that damaged the refractory of the convent was a Nazi bomb or a British Bomb.

Restoration continued. In the 1970s a twenty-one year effort put a new face on the painting by removing the old paint and providing it a climate controlled environment. The *new and improved* painting was more like the original, at least according to the restorer. Detractors say otherwise. Regardless, the painting was open to the public in 1999.

As evidence of daVinci's attention to detail is the single vanishing point of the painting. It is said that he used a nail at the point of infinity with a string attached so that he could see the perspective of anything depicted. It is one of the best examples in the art world of a single-point perspective. This assures that the eyes always focus on Jesus. The nail and string allowed da Vinci to be able to paint an exact perspective on each element of the painting.

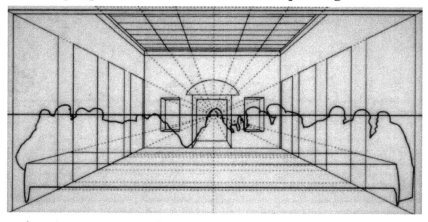

Another interesting fact, the painting was copied a number of times. Da Vinci contemporaries, Giampietrino (probably Giavonni Pietro Rizzoli), Andrea Solari, and Cesare da Sesto painted exact copies. They were presumed to be da Vinci's assistants. These copies are on display at the Royal Academy of Art in London, Leonardo da Vinci Museum in Belgium, and the Church of Saint Ambrogio in Switzerland respectively. However, their copies were instrumental in recent restoration efforts especially the one by Giampietrino which was the main guide.

Stylized copies by Salvador Dali and Andy Warhol lead the list of contemporary copies. The Last Supper was an example used by Mel Brooks in his parody movie, *History of the World, Part 1.*

It is also at the top of the list of paintings that have been parodied. The Royal Academy of Arts list it in their top ten. Some of the notable parodies include: The Fast Supper with Ronald McDonald in the center surrounded by other advertising icons including the Burger King, Colonel Sanders, Taco Bell's Chihuahua and Wendy; The Last Breakfast with cereal characters; The First Supper with women from around the world; The Last Supper with South Park characters, one with Star Wars characters, one with Peanut characters, one with Marvel Comics characters, one with Smurf characters, one with dog breeds, one with Popeye's characters, one with Legos characters, one with Ace playing card characters at a craps table, one with Muppets characters, one with Disney characters with Mickey in the center, scientists Last Supper with Einstein in the center, NBA stars, Lesbian Last Supper with Ellen in the center, Warner Bros characters with Bugs in the center, another has the original participants with everyone looking at a cell phone and the last one on my list, and maybe the most disrespectful to Christians is Jesus taking a selfie.

La Cène de Jean Sulpice

A caricature of Bagutta Prize ceremony by Pavel Gromov

"As a well spent day brings happy sleep, so a well spent life brings happy death."

Leonardo da Vinci

ALL WRONG
ARTISTIC LICENSE OR ULTERIOR MOTIVE

There are so many inaccuracies in the painting that it is reasonably correct to say the painting is all wrong.

To begin with first century dinners were never at long tables, and participants did not sit in chairs—they reclined on their left side on pillows or mats. The accepted way to dine was to eat only with the right hand. Why? Because the left hand was reserved for personal hygiene use. Plainly said after relieving themselves they wiped with their bare left hand. Even today it is considered bad manners to offer the left hand to shake in Arabic countries.

A first century dinner would follow the Roman custom because the Roman Empire occupied Palestine. In Roman times participants would recline at an open square table—positions on the outside of the three sides. This open square table is called a triclinium. The Romans adopted this from the Greeks. The open center mades it easier for the servants to serve the food and allowed for easier conversations among the participants. There are accepted seating positioning at the table. The host sits in the second position on the left side. The most honored guest would sit on the host's left. The youngest guest on the host's right. The servant would sit in the last position on the right side. The likely use of the triclinium at the Last Supper can be confirmed by references in the New Testament of the KJV Bible. (John 13:23, Matthew 26:23, and John 13:24). By understanding the configuration of the table and the customary seating standards, and with the help of the Gospels, we can place four of the thirteen people present at the Last Supper—Jesus, John, Judas, and Peter.

Since Jesus was the host, He would have sat in the second seat on the right side of the triclinium, called the *Lectus Imus*. John, the youngest of the Disciples, would have been on His right. That is documented by John 13:23, *"Now there was leaning on Jesus' bosom one of his disciples, whom Jesus loved."* That was how John generally referenced himself.

Considering how they were reclining, the only place for John to be is on Jesus right. Judas was on His left. That is documented by Matthew 26:23, *" He that dippeth his hand with me in the dish, the same shall betray me."* Again, based on how they were reclining at the table, only the person on Jesus' left could physically dip from the same dish. Hence, Judas was on Jesus' left.

It is interesting that the position on the host's left was considered the honored position *locus consularis* or chief consular, while Peter's

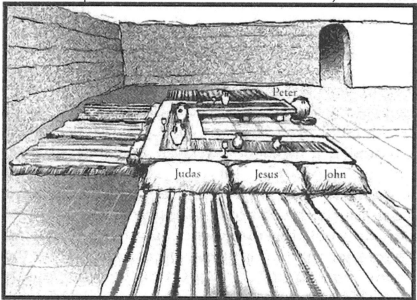

position, *seat of the servant*, is that he was designated as Bishop of Rome or *servant of the servants of Christ*.

It is generally accepted by theologians and historians that the Last Supper was the Seder meal served as a part of Passover week. Seder is the second day of Passover week and commemorates the flight of the Jewish people from bondage of the Egyptians. In considering the dates of Hebrew feasts, it is important to remember that the new day begins at sunset. Seder is celebrated after sunset. Seder is a requirement of the Passover week celebration called the Feast of Unleavened Bread. Additionally, there is a prescribed format of the meal and a narrative for what the various dishes symbolize.

The Hebrew calendar is a true lunar calendar in that a month is the time between new moons or 29.53059 days. The Julian calendar was established in 45 BC by Julius Caesar and revised by Pope Gregory XIII in 1582 AD as the Gregorian calendar—Which we continue to use to this day. Both the Julian and Gregorian calendar are solar calendars.

The lunar calendar coincides with the seasons (please see the appendix for additional information). Passover is celebrated on the 14th day of the first month (Nisan). Seder on Nisan 15. Although there is no documentation, there is some agreement that Jesus was crucified on April 3rd in the year 33 AD. Oxford University scientists, Colin J. Humphreys and W.G. Waddington, propose that Jesus could only have been crucified on April 3rd 33 AD. Their research was based on astronomical history. The report was published in the British Journal Nature. Using that as the benchmark, the Last Supper would have been on Wednesday April 1st in the year 33 AD.

None of the Gospels document the date of the last supper, but if we superimpose Hebrew tradition with current calendars, the Seder meal/Last Supper would have been celebrated on April 1 which is Nisan 14 in the year 33 AD (the year 3793 on the Hebrew calendar.) That date is corroborated by recent discoveries of Essens, Sumarian, and Zealot lunar calendars.

"While I thought I was learning to live, I have been learning how to die."

~Leonardo da Vinci

THE EUCHARIST AND THE BIBLICAL ACCOUNT
SURROUNDING THE LAST SUPPER

The Last Supper was a pivotal point in the life of Jesus and essential to the continuation of His ministry. Pivotal also for Christianity and Roman Catholics. Eucharist (from the Greek *eucharistia* or thanksgiving) along with Baptism are the sacraments documented in the Bible.

Roman Catholics celebrate the Last Supper as one of the Luminous Mysteries of the Rosary. The Fifth Luminous Mystery calls on Catholics to contemplate Jesus' institution of the Sacrament of the Holy Eucharist at the Last Supper. Wikipedia says the Last Supper celebration "has evolved into a more formal worship service and has become codified as the Mass." The mass of the Lord's Supper is also called "A Service of Worship for Maundy Thursday."

The Mass stresses three aspects of the event:
1. the institution of the Eucharist
2. the institution of the ministerial priesthood
3. the commandment of brotherly love through the washing of feet.

The Liturgy of the Word consists of the reading of:

1. Exodus chapter 12 verses 1–8, 11–14, a description of the original Passover celebration
2. Psalms chapter 115, the thanksgiving for being saved
3. Corinthians chapter 11 verses 23–26, Paul's account of what Jesus did at His Last Supper
4. John chapter 13 verses 1–15, John's account of how Jesus washed the feet of the disciples before the meal as an example of how they should treat each other.

In addition to the Catholic celebration, Lutheran, Anglican, Methodist, and certain Presbyterian and Congregational churches celebrate services similar to the Mass of the Last Supper on Maundy Thursday.

The Eastern Orthodox calls the celebration "the Divine Liturgy" and is considered a Sacrament of the Eucharist. On "Holy Thursday" women of the church dye Easter eggs for the family. They are usually red to symbolize Jesus' blood. A red egg is ofter baked in the traditional "tsoureki" bread which symbolizes Jesus' body. The special bread is made to be eaten on Easter Sunday symbolizing the body and blood of the Eucharist. The church service usually includes the reading of:

1. Exodus chapter 19 verses 10–19, Moses consecrates the people in advance of the 10 commandments
2. Psalm chapter 58, "deliver me from mine enemies, O God defend me from them that rise against me"
3. Job chapter 38 verses 1–21 and chapter 43 verses 1–5, God reveals Himself to Job
4. Isaiah chapter 50 verses 4–11, suffering servant song.

Early Christians observed the Last Supper as a full meal called the "Agape Feast" or Love Feast. It was usually celebrated on Sunday which became known as the Lord's Day. The meal was to celebrate

1. the resurrection
2. the appearance to the disciples on the Emmaus Road

3. His appearance to Thomas
4. and Pentecost, all of which took place on Sunday.

Christians consider the Last Supper as the beginning of the New Covenant as predicted by Jeremiah in chapter 31 verses 31–34

"Behold, the days are coming, declares the Lord, when I will make a new covenant with the house of Israel and the house of Judah, not like the covenant that I made with their fathers on the day when I took them by the hand to bring them out of the land of Egypt, my covenant that they broke, though I was their husband, declares the Lord. For this is the covenant that I will make with the house of Israel after those days, declares the Lord: I will put my law within them, and I will write it on their hearts. And I will be their God, and they shall be my people."

"Nature is the source of all knowledge. She has her own logic, her own laws, she has no effect without cause nor invention without necessity."

~Leonardo da Vinci

Only three of the gospels present the story of the last meal but even in these descriptions we often miss the depth of meaning provided. Much is to be learned by harmonizing them. We know that the Last Supper took place as a part of the Passover celebration, most likely the Seder meal.

We pick up the story in Mark chapter 14 verses 13–16, where Jesus directs two of the disciples to:

> *"Go ye into the city (Jerusalem), and there shall meet you a man bearing a pitcher of water: follow him. And wheresoever he shall go in, say ye to the good man of the house, The Master saith, Where is the guest chamber, where I shall eat the Passover with my disciples? And he will shew you a large upper room furnished and prepared: there make ready for us. And his disciples went forth, and came into the city, and found as He had said unto them: and they made ready the Passover."*

Jesus said go find a man bearing a pitcher of water. The importance of this statement is that carrying water was a specific duty of the women. Mark continues:

> *And in the evening He cometh with the twelve. And as they sat and did eat, Jesus said, Verily I say unto you, One of you which eateth with me shall betray me."*

Matthew chapter 26 verses 17–19 says it this way:

> *"Now the first day of the feast of unleavened bread the disciples came to Jesus, saying unto him, Where wilt thou that we prepare for thee to eat the Passover? And he said, Go into the city to such a man, and say unto him, The Master saith, My time is at hand; I will keep the Passover at thy house with my disciples. And the disciples did as Jesus had appointed them; and they made ready the Passover."*

Luke chapter 22 verses 7–13 confirmed that the two disciples sent were John and Peter.

> *"Then came the day of unleavened bread, when the Passover (lamb) must be killed. And He sent Peter and John, saying, Go and prepare us the Passover, that we may eat. And they said unto him, Where wilt thou that we prepare? And he said unto them, Behold, when ye are entered into the city, there shall a man meet you, bearing a pitcher of water; follow him into the house where he entereth in. And ye shall say unto the good man of the house, The Master saith unto thee, Where is the guest chamber, where I shall eat the Passover with my disciples? And he shall shew you a large upper room furnished: there make ready. And they went, and found as He had said unto them: and they made ready the Passover."*

John reported none of the details. John chapter 13 verse 1 states simply:

> *"Now before the feast of the Passover, when Jesus knew that his hour was come that He should depart out of this world unto the Father, having loved his own which were in the world, he loved them unto the end."*

A close-up view of Jesus in da Vinci's painting suggests the sacrament of the Eucharist. He is clearly gesturing to the cup and the bread. The "Lord's Supper" or "Holy Communion" is a celebration in Christian churches. The Gospels of Matthew, Mark, and Luke present similar stories.

Matthew quotes Jesus as he described the elements of the Eucharist in chapter 26 verses 26–29:

> *"And as they were eating, Jesus took bread, and blessed it, and brake it, and gave it to the disciples, and said, Take, eat; this*

is my body. And he took the cup, and gave thanks, and gave it to them, saying, Drink ye all of it; For this is my blood of the new testament, which is shed for many for the remission of sins. But I say unto you, I will not drink henceforth of this fruit of the vine, until that day when I drink it new with you in my Father's kingdom."

Mark verified the service in Chapter 14 verses 22–25:

"And as they did eat, Jesus took bread, and blessed, and brake it, and gave to them, and said, Take, eat: this is my body. And he took the cup, and when he had given thanks, he gave it to them: and they all drank of it. And he said unto them, This is my blood of the new testament, which is shed for many. Verily I say unto you, I will drink no more of the fruit of the vine, until that day that I drink it new in the kingdom of God."

Luke's description is found in Luke chapter 22 verses 14–20:

"And when the hour was come, he sat down, and the twelve apostles with him. And he said unto them, With desire I have desired to eat this Passover with you before I suffer: For I say unto you, I will not any more eat thereof, until it be fulfilled in the kingdom of God. And he took the cup, and gave thanks, and said, Take this, and divide it among yourselves: For I say unto you, I will not drink of the fruit of the vine, until the kingdom of God shall come. And he took bread, and gave thanks, and brake it, and gave unto them, saying, This is my body which is given for you: this do in remembrance of me. Likewise also the cup after supper, saying, This cup is the new testament in my blood, which is shed for you."

The gospel of John provides a different view of the Last Supper. It focuses on the foot washing. However, following Judas' departure, the Gospel of John chapter 13 verses 34–35 provides Jesus' new commandment:

> *"A new commandment I give unto you, That ye love one another; as I have loved you, that ye also love one another. By this shall all men know that ye are my disciples, if ye have love one to another."*

Then, in chapters 14–16, John records a long sermon by Jesus in which he gives instruction for His followers. John chapter 17 verses 1–26 is generally known as Jesus' farewell prayer to God.

> *"These words spake Jesus, and lifted up his eyes to heaven, and said, Father, the hour is come; glorify thy Son, that thy Son also may glorify thee: As thou hast given him power over all flesh, that he should give eternal life to as many as thou hast given him. And this is life eternal, that they might know thee the only true God, and Jesus Christ, whom thou hast sent. I have glorified thee on the earth: I have finished the work which thou gavest me to do. And now, O Father, glorify thou me with thine own self with the glory which I had with thee before the world was. I have manifested thy name unto the men which thou gavest me out of the world: thine they were, and thou gavest them me; and they have kept thy word. Now they have known that all things whatsoever thou hast given me are of thee. For I have given unto them the words which thou gavest me; and they have received them, and have known surely that I came out from thee, and they have believed that thou didst send me. I pray for them: I pray not for the world, but for them which thou hast given me; for they are thine. And all mine are thine, and thine are mine; and I am glorified in them. And now I am no more in the world, but these are in the world, and I come to thee. Holy Father, keep through thine own name those whom thou hast given me, that they may be one, as we are. While I was with them in the world, I kept them in thy name:*

those that thou gavest me I have kept, and none of them is lost, but the son of perdition; that the scripture might be fulfilled. And now come I to thee; and these things I speak in the world, that they might have my joy fulfilled in themselves. I have given them thy word; and the world hath hated them, because they are not of the world, even as I am not of the world. I pray not that thou shouldest take them out of the world, but that thou shouldest keep them from the evil. They are not of the world, even as I am not of the world. Sanctify them through thy truth: thy word is truth. As thou hast sent me into the world, even so have I also sent them into the world. And for their sakes I sanctify myself, that they also might be sanctified through the truth. Neither pray I for these alone, but for them also which shall believe on me through their word; That they all may be one; as thou, Father, art in me, and I in thee, that they also may be one in us: that the world may believe that thou hast sent me. And the glory which thou gavest me I have given them; that they may be one, even as we are one: I in them, and thou in me, that they may be made perfect in one; and that the world may know that thou hast sent me, and hast loved them, as thou hast loved me. Father, I will that they also, whom thou hast given me, be with me where I am; that they may behold my glory, which thou hast given me: for thou lovedst me before the foundation of the world. O righteous Father, the world hath not known thee: but I have known thee, and these have known that thou hast sent me. And I have declared unto them thy name, and will declare it: that the love wherewith thou hast loved me may be in them, and I in them.

In chapter 11 verses 23–26 of his first epistle to the Christian in Corinth, the apostle Paul seems to codify the Last Supper sacrament:

"For I have received of the Lord that which also I delivered unto you, that the Lord Jesus the same night in which he was

betrayed took bread: And when he had given thanks, he brake it, and said, Take, eat: this is my body, which is broken for you: this do in remembrance of me. After the same manner also he took the cup, when he had supped, saying, this cup is the new testament in my blood: this do ye, as oft as ye drink it, in remembrance of me. For as often as ye eat this bread, and drink this cup, ye do shew the Lord's death till he come."

"Where there is shouting, there is no true knowledge."
~Leonardo da Vinci

LEONARDO DA VINCI
THE MAN

Leonardo da Vinci (Leonardo di ser Piero da Vinci) was born in Anchiano, Italy, August 15, 1452. Wikipedia calls him a *polymath*. Plainly stated, "a person with wide-ranging knowledge or learning".

Today he would be called a Renaissance Man, which he was and easily he was the first. He is listed as a painter, draughtsman, engineer, scientist, theorist, inventor, sculptor, and architect. Looking at the drawings of ideas that we see and use everyday, it is clear that he was a man ahead of his time. His *Codex Atlanticus* included design drawings of an airplane, a helicopter, a submarine, a tank, a parachute, a steam engine and a number of other inventions that are in use today.

In his biography of da Vinci, Walter Issacson points out that da Vinci was "a societal misfit: illegitimate, gay, vegetarian, left-handed, easily distracted, and, at times, heretical." Researchers at Thomas Jefferson University say he was probably dyslexic. He was minimally schooled in math and writing. He was never trained and completely unwilling to separate science from art.

As an artist he was essentially self-trained. He apprenticed with Andrea del Varrocchio, a Florentine sculpture, artist, and goldsmith. As was the custom, da Vinci painted a portion of Varrocchio's *The Baptism of Christ*. The angel painted by da Vinci, second from the left in the painting, is both technically and creatively different from the rest of the painting. The painting was completed in 1475 AD. It was said that Varrocchio gave up painting when he saw da Vinci's work.

His drawings show his geophysical, botanical, hydrological and aerological research that established his "visible cosmology" goal. The art of seeing is easy when solving problems. Knowing how to see is the key to unlocking the secrets of the visible world. It is easy to understand that he favored the irrefutable facts from experience

(sapper vedere). Da Vinci's use of this research is evident in The Last Supper. Plato's philosophies and Neo-Platonic thought, seeing the world beyond the material world and the idea of perfection and beauty, is obvious in da Vinci's paintings. Even the structure of the images in The Last Supper reflect the golden sections of Platonic Proportions. Da Vinci believed that the painter who is endowed with the subtle powers of perception and the ability to paint them is the best qualified person to achieve true knowledge since he can observe and reproduce the world around him.

"There are three classes of people: those who see. Those see when they are shown. Those who do not see."

~Leonardo da Vinci

He was quoted as saying, "When I saw the hint of a smile come across someone's lips, I tried to fathom her inner mysteries." Such it was with *Mona Lisa's* mysterious smile. Although never confirmed, the model for the *Mona Lisa* was believed to be Caterina, a sixteen-year-old orphan.

At age 24 (c. 1476), da Vinci designed a self-propelled vehicle, certainly the forerunner of the automobile. Twenty-first century computer modelers have assembled a three dimensional, full size model exactly by da Vinci's drawing specifications. It actually works.

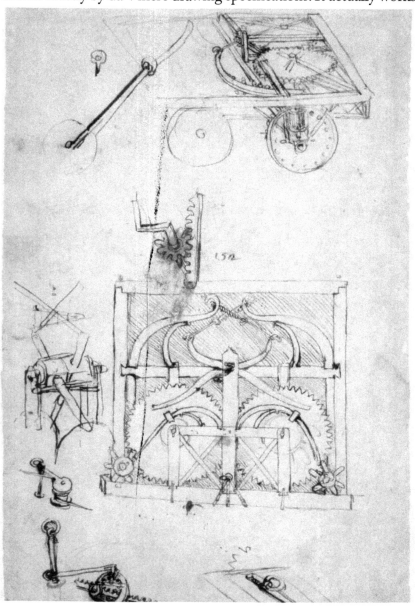

The vehicle is sometimes called the "clockworks car" because it is propelled by a spring similar to the system that runs a windup clock. The 5´ x 5.5´ vehicle has three wheels and can travel 131 feet before the spring has to be rewound. He also designed the ball bearing some twenty years later. Full size models of da Vinci's self-propelled vehicle are on display at the Museum of History and Science in Florence, Italy and at the Toyota Museum in Tokyo, Japan.

He was overlooked in the list of painters considered for the Sistine Chapel provided to the Pope by Lorenzo de' Medici. By 1483, he had left Florence and established his own studio in Milan. Now thirty years old and living in Milan, he wrote a letter to Ludovico Sforza, Duke of Milan, offering his service as a military engineer. He also mentioned he was a painter.

Da Vinci was employed by Sforza and designed a chariot fitted with enormous whirling blades that would slice men in half or cut off their legs, a multi-barrel machine gun, and a colossal crossbow.

In 1495, da Vinci began work on *The Last Supper*. It was finished in 1498. The following year, Sforza was deposed by Louis XII, King of France. Since the painting was painted on the wall of the convent, they were unable to pry it off the wall.

"Simplicity is the ultimate sophistication."
~Leonardo da Vinci

Mystery seemed to follow Leonardo da Vinci. There was a feud between da Vinci and Michelangelo. It apparently originated when da Vinci objection to Michelangelo's *David* because of it's exposed penis. "It needs a decent ornament."

Da Vinci prevailed, and the penis was covered for some forty years. Michelangelo returned to Florence in 1506, and daVinci decided to move back to Milan taking with him the painting *Mona Lisa* that he had started in 1503. It was discovered in his studio when he died in May of 1519 at sixty-seven years of age.

The Mona Lisa's smile is a source of mystery even today. Da Vinci was known to dissect cadavers in order to draw studies of lip muscles. These studies are likely related to Mona Lisa's famous smile. It is even said to contain hidden symbols. The smile seems to change even though the paint does not. Da Vinci was a master of the use of shadow. The edges of the smile are in shadow and slightly out of focus. Research by the Smith-Kettlewell Eye Research Institute in San Francisco associates Christopher Tyler and Leonid Kontsevich say the smile changes because of the random way the human visual system works. Harvard University's Margaret Livingstone says that the edges of the smile are most easily seen by the peripheral vision, and this could result is changes of the look of the smile.

Other possibilities presented are that she is pregnant, so the smile is a happy one; or that she has a unhappy marriage, and the smile is a sad one. One of the more questionable is offered by Dr. Lillian Schwartz of Bell Laboratories. She suggests that Mona Lisa is smiling because the artist is joking with the viewers. The subject is actually a self-portrait and not the pretty woman it seems to be.

Even the name, Mona Lisa, carries da Vinci's mystery. Mona is translated as "noble" or "aristocrat" in Italian and is thought to be a derivation of Madonna (virgin Mary). Lisa is a diminutive of Elisa derived from Hebrew "El Ischa" meaning "God is health."

The same mystery continues to surround da Vinci even today. He has been sited as a member of a number of secret societies. In their book, *Holy Blood, Holy Grail*, Michael Baigent, Richard Leigh, and Henry Lincoln present the information that da Vinci, along with Sir Isaac Newton, Victor Hugo, and Claude Debussy were Grand Masters of a secret society called the Priory of Sion. That idea was propagated by Dan Brown in his novel, *The Da Vinci Code*. The list of Grand Masters of the Priory of Sion was discovered by British Broadcasting Company (BBC) investigators in a document, *Dossiers Secrets*, found in the Bibliotheque nationale de France (Frances' National Library). The document is also surrounded by mystery. It is supposed to document a connection of the Priory to the Merovingian dynasty (French kings 457–751 AD). However, the document was placed in the Library in the 1950s by Pierre Plantard ostensibly linking Plantard to the Merovingins.

Other suggestions link da Vinci's name to the Free Masons, the Literati, Knights Templar, the Rosicrucians, the Cathars, the Elders of Zion, and the Golden Dawn.

As with most mysteries, concrete evidence is difficult to find.

"The truth of things is the chief nutriment of superior intellects."
~Leonardo Da Vinci

A COMMENT ON DYSLEXIA

It seems logical. Da Vinci joins an elite group of people believed to have been dyslexic. There is no way to be certain, but he shares many traits with a number of dyslexic artists, including Pablo Picasso and Andy Warhol, and scientists and inventors, including Alexander Graham Bell, Albert Einstein, and Thomas Edison. Dyslexia expert Maryanne Wolf said, "as a researcher working with hundreds of children and adults with dyslexia, I am convinced that Leonardo da Vinci was dyslexic," in a Smithsonian interview.

Dyslexia has long been recognized as a condition with deficiencies that had to be overcome. Recently, however, researchers are adding that dyslexic individuals have added strengths that maybe considered gifts. Many *out of the box* thinkers are dyslexic. They are able to see things from different perspectives due to their dyslexia.

In their book, *Dyslexic Advantages*, Brock and Fernette Eide call one of the dyslexic advantages "interconnected reasoning" or the ability recognize relationships across disciplines.

"I love those who can smile in trouble, who can gather strength from distress, and grow brave by reflection. 'Tis the business of little minds to shrink, but they whose heart is firm, and whose conscience approves their conduct, will pursue their principles unto death."

~Leonardo da Vinci

Hosting a Seder
by D. T. Lancaster

A Big Mitzvah

So you've decided to do a Passover seder meal! Good. The celebration of the Passover with unleavened bread and bitter herbs is a commandment. Even more, it is a commandment of the Master to do this in remembrance of Him! You are preparing to keep one of the Master's most sacred instructions to his disciples! God will bless you as you keep his Torah and His son's command. May the Lord bless your home.

Calendar Dates

The first step to keeping the Feast of Unleavened Bread is to acknowledge it. Using a Jewish Calendar (https://www.hebcal.com), find when the 15th of Nissan falls this year. Remember that a biblical day begins at sunset. The evening that begins the 15th of Nissan is the beginning of the festival and the seder night. (Hint: The 15th is always a full moon.)

Unleavened Bread is seven days long. The first and seventh days are sabbaths. This means that no work should be performed (except food preparation) from sunset to sunset on the first and seventh days of the festival. The intervening days are not sabbaths, but they are still regarded as part of the festival.

Inviting Guests

When hosting a seder, it is a good idea to invite guests. The seder is a celebration of our shared salvation. The haggadah declares, "Whoever is hungry—let him come and eat! Whoever is needy—let him come and celebrate the Passover!" Our brothers and sisters are hungry for Torah. Our brothers and sisters are impoverished of the Master's words and ways. Our homes should be open to anyone and everyone who shows an interest in learning the ways of Torah and the salvation of the Master.

Leaven

Prior to sunset, twenty-four hours before the seder, products containing chametz (wheat, barley, spelt, oats, rye) should be removed from the household. They should be consumed, sold, given away or disposed of before the festival. Sunset of seder night is the absolute deadline for removing the leaven. For the duration of the seven days, no product containing yeast can be eaten or brought into the home. It is a commandment to eat unleavened bread—that is, matzah—on each of the seven days. Eat at least one piece a day. The spiritual lessons of the matzah and the cleansing out of the old leaven run deep through our scriptures. The haggadah will lead you through the ritual cleansing of your home.

For more specific information on leaven, and chametz and how to remove it, please read our "Leaven and Passover" article.

The Seder

Beginning at sunset on the evening that begins the 15th day of Nissan, everyone is enjoined to participate in a seder meal. The seder celebrates Israel's redemption from Egypt. Bitter herbs, unleavened bread, and the fruit of the vine are enjoyed while the story of the Exodus is retold. In temple times, lamb was eaten. Because there is no temple today, it is forbidden to make a sacrifice. Therefore lamb is never eaten at a seder. To do so would be to imply a sacrifice had been made! The seder meal simultaneously tells the story of the Exodus from Egypt and the Last Supper and Passion of the Master. It contains within it the elements of communion, and it is a remembrance of Him.

Set Order

Seder means "set order." A Passover seder is called a seder because there is a set order to the rituals and elements of the meal. There are fifteen consecutive steps which constitute a full seder.

1. *Kaddesh* (Sanctification): Declaration of the sanctity of the Festival over the first cup of wine. The first cup.
2. *Ur'chatz* (Hand Washing): A ritual purification.
3. *Karpas* (Dipping Vegetables): A reminder of the tears of Egypt.
4. *Yachatz* (Breaking of Bread): Breaking unleavened bread, hiding the afikomen.
5. *Maggid* (Telling the Story): Telling the story of the deliverance from Egypt. The second cup.
6. *Rachtzah* (Hand Washing): Washing hands before eating bread.
7. *Motzi* (Blessing for Bread): The blessing before eating bread.
8. *Matzah* (Eating Unleavened Bread): The blessing for keeping the commandment to eat unleavened bread.
9. *Maror* (Eating Bitter Herbs): The blessing for keeping the commandment to eat bitter herbs.
10. *Korech* (Unleavened Bread With Bitter Herbs): Unleavened bread and bitter herbs are eaten together to keep the literal command, "You shall eat unleavened bread with bitter herbs."
11. *Shulchan Orech* (Setting the Table): The regular meal is eaten.
12. *Tzafun* (Eating the afikomen): The afikomen, the hidden unleavened bread, is eaten.
13. *Barech* (Grace After Meals): After eating, the Grace After Meals is prayed. The third cup.
14. *Hallel* (Praise Psalms): Psalm 113–118 are sung or recited. The fourth cup.
15. *Nirtzah* (Conclusion): The seder is concluded.

Haggadah

The haggadah is the booklet which guides you through these fifteen steps. Haggadah means *telling*, and the telling of the Exodus from Egypt is the main purpose of the Passover seder. Disciples also use the seder to retell the story of the Master's last supper with them. We recommend the *Vine of David Haggadah*.

A haggadah is meant as a guide to this telling. It should be regarded as a rough outline, not a finished product. The host of the seder should feel free to improvise, to condense long passages, to skip certain sections, to linger on certain passages, or to rework the material spontaneously. The important thing at a seder is that it is enjoyable. It is to be a time of joy.

While the haggadah does guide you through the seder, it is important that the participants feel free to interrupt the haggadah with songs, hymns, and choruses. The seder is a time of joy. The haggadah is only a guide, not an iron rule! Every seder is uniquely different.

A Meal for Children

The most important guests at a seder are the children. The intention of the seder is to retell the story of God's salvation to the next generation. If the seder becomes boring for the children and they lose interest, then the whole exercise is futile. The host of the seder must do everything in his or her power to keep the children engaged and interested as the seder progresses.

Homes with young children should consider telling the *Maggid* (the story of the Exodus) on a child's level. The haggadah tells it in midrashic form, on a sage's level, which may not be appropriate for young children. You might consider shortening the Hallel and praying only the first blessing of *Barech* (Grace After Meals). Introduce games and amusements to keep the children engaged. (A reward for finding the afikomen can be a big incentive to stay at the table!)

The meal should be reverent, but don't forget to have fun!

Strange Customs

Because the seder meal is actually an ancient ritual which pre-dates Christianity by 1,400 years, there are many customs in a seder meal which are unfamiliar to us. For example, at ancient banquets people did not sit in chairs, they reclined on pillows around a floor-level table. That is why we read in the gospels, "the Master was reclining at the table." As a remembrance of "reclining," everyone leans to the left when drinking the four cups or when eating the unleavened bread or bitter herbs. Dipping vegetables and washing hands before bread are also ancient customs from the days of the Master.

Four Cups

Through the course of the seder meal, four cups of wine or grape juice are consumed. The four cups correspond to the four expressions of redemption that God spoke to Israel in Exodus 6:6,7.

The Cup Of Salvation

The Sages accordingly ordained four cups to be drank on the eve of Passover to correspond with these four expressions in order to fulfill the verse found in Psalms 116:13: "I will lift up the cup of salvation, and call upon the name of the Lord." (*Shemot Rabbah* 6.4)

Preparing for the Seder

In addition to cleansing the house of leaven and preparing a festive meal, there are some ritual foods that need to be prepared for a seder. Five items are arranged on a large plate. This plate is referred to as the seder plate.

On The Seder Plate

Shankbone: A Piece of Roasted Lamb Shankbone (a chicken neck is often substituted).

The shankbone of a lamb is in remembrance of the Passover Lamb sacrifice. Since there no longer is a temple, there is no sacrifice, but the shankbone serves as a reminder that in ancient times a roasted lamb was served.

Roasted Egg: A Roasted Egg. (Some boil an egg in dark tea to make it look roasted.)

The roasted egg is also placed on the seder plate as a remembrance of the additional sacrifices that were made at Passover. These additional peace offering sacrifices were also eaten on the Festival. Traditionally, the First Born at the table eat the roasted egg during Shulchan Orech in order to remember how God passed over the first born of Israel when he struck Egypt.

Vegetable: Celery or Parsley.

The Vegetable is dipped into saltwater and eaten during Karpas. The salty taste is meant to remind the participants of the tears that were wept in Egypt.

Charoset: Apple-nut mix.

The Charoset is a brown mush mixture that is meant to look like the mortar used in making bricks for the Egyptians. Actually it is a sweet fruit salad that serves as an antidote to the heat and pain and distaste of the bitter herbs. (See Recipe below).

Bitter Herbs: Whole Romaine Lettuce Leaves and Grated Horseradish.

The Romaine Lettuce Leaves and Grated Horseradish constitute the bitter herbs that the Torah commands are to be eaten along with unleavened bread at a seder meal. They are a remembrance of the bitterness of Egypt.

On The Table

In addition to the ritual items on the seder plate, you will also need the following things to successfully complete your seder:

Wine: Enough grape juice or wine for each participant to drink four full cups.

A linen: A linen to wrap the afikomen in.

A large linen: A linen napkin to wrap the three whole unleavened bread-matzah crackers in.

Unleavened bread: Enough unleavened bread (matzah crackers) for each participant to eat a full piece.

Saltwater: A bowl of salt water for dipping vegetables.

A basin of water with pitcher: For hand washing.

A towel: For hand drying.

Candles: Two or more candles for candle-lighting.

A Sweet Remembrance of Bitterness

On the Passover seder plate, the charoset is said to symbolize the mortar used by the slaves in Egypt. When charoset is properly made, it should look like mortar: a substance with a muddy, mush-like consistency.

Charoset serves more than just a symbolic purpose on the seder plate. It is used as a sweet antidote to the bitter herbs we are commanded to eat. The charoset is used to sweeten the romaine lettuce of Maror and to kill the heat and pain of the horseradish in Korech.

Charoset Recipe

2 medium-sized apples

1/2 cup chopped walnuts

1/2-1 teaspoon cinnamon

2-3 tablespoon honey (or sweeten to taste)

Peel and core the apples. Then chop or grate into mush. Mix in the rest of the ingredients. Giving everything a spin in the food processor helps to make it into a mushy, mortar-like substance.

Although the bricks in Egypt were made with straw, it is a universal charoset tradition to abstain from adding straw to the recipe in remembrance of the passage that says:

Remember, do not mix in any straw, as it is written, Then the slave drivers and the foremen went out and said to the people, "This is what Pharaoh says: 'I will not give you any more straw.'" (Exodus 5:10)

"Poor is the pupil who does not surpass his master."
~Leonardo da Vinci

LAST SUPPER OR LAST SEDER?
BY D. T. LANCASTER

Was Jesus' Last Supper a Passover Seder? On what day did Yeshua die, and did He celebrate a Passover Seder with His disciples or not?

Yeshua died on a Friday, but what day of the month was it? And by "day of the month," I mean, on what day of the biblical calendar did He die? Was it the thirteenth day of Nissan, the fourteenth day of Nissan, or the fifteenth day of Nissan? Maybe this seems like a trivial question, but every year around Passover, I receive questions about the timing of the passion week. People want to understand how the story of the death and resurrection of Yeshua fits together with the biblical calendar and the festival of Passover.

The question stems from a discrepancy between the way the Gospel of John and the gospels of Matthew, Mark, and Luke tell the story of the Last Supper and the day of the crucifixion. Some Bible teachers try to smooth over the discrepancy, cover it up, or outright deny its existence, but that does not really help the situation at all. Christian readers who are not familiar with the details of the celebration of Passover and the timing of the biblical calendar might never notice the problem at all. Thanks to ignorance about the Torah, most readers do not see the conflict.

John's Chronology

When reading the Gospels from a Jewish perspective, however, the problem becomes obvious. In the Gospel of John, Yeshua has his Last Supper the night before the sacrifice of the Passover lambs (Korban Pesach). In other words, Yeshua conducts the Last Supper a full twenty-four hours before the Jewish people sit down to eat a Passover Seder meal. He is crucified the next day as the Passover lambs are sacrificed in the Temple courts. That night at sunset, the holy day sabbath (Yom Tov) of the first day of Passover begins. It corresponded that year with the weekly seventh-day Sabbath. In the Gospel of John, Nicodemus and Joseph of Arimathea close the tomb of Yeshua as the Yom Tov of Nisan 15 begins, right at the time when everyone would be sitting down to eat a Passover Seder meal. For that reason, the Gospel of John does not refer to the Last Supper (John 13–17) as a Passover meal at all. It makes no mention of Passover except to state that the meal took place "before the festival of the Passover" (John 13:1).

The Synoptic Chronology

The Synoptic Gospels of Matthew, Mark, and Luke tell a totally different story. John says that the meal took place "before the festival of Passover," but in the Synoptic Gospels, the Passover is underway. In the Synoptic Gospels, Yeshua sends two disciples to sacrifice a Passover lamb and prepare an upper room for a Passover Seder meal. It's the fourteenth day of Nisan. That night, the fifteenth day begins at sunset. The Yom Tov has already begun when they sit down to recline at a Passover Seder meal together. Yeshua says, "I have eagerly desired to eat this Passover with you." The Synoptic Gospels depict the entire meal as a Passover Seder.

The Synoptic telling of the story implies that the Yom Tov of Nisan 15 (the special sabbath of the first day of Passover) has already begun and that the Last Supper is a seder. Accordingly, Yeshua is arrested on Yom Tov, tried on Yom Tov, brought before Pilate on Yom Tov, traded for Barabbas on Yom Tov, crucified on Yom Tov, removed from the cross on Yom Tov, and prepared and buried on Yom Tov. Moreover, a member the Sanhedrin purchases a shroud and supplies for his burial on a Yom Tov. As the tomb closes, the second day of Passover begins, coinciding with the onset of the weekly Sabbath.

Attempted Solutions

Scholars have recognized and puzzled over the discrepancy for centuries. Over the years, many commentators have made valiant attempts to reconcile and harmonize John's version of events with that of the Synoptic Gospels. Most New Testament scholars today, however, have abandoned the quest. They are content to admit that John tells the story one way and the Synoptic Gospels tell it another way. That's no fun. So let's take a look at how people have tried to harmonize this problem in the past.

In his voluminous commentary, *The Death of the Messiah*, Raymond Brown categorizes and catalogues various attempts at explaining, harmonizing, and reconciling the discrepancy. Harmonizations attempt to rearrange the sequence. These usually accept the synoptic version and try to force John's version to agree with it, but it requires them to ignore or explain away passages like John 18:28 which mentions that, when the Master stood before Pilate, the priesthood would not enter the Praetorium because they did not want to become unclean and forfeit their opportunity to eat the Passover lamb. In other words, the Passover Seder had not happened yet, and it was going to happen that night.

One theory proposes that the Galileans celebrated Passover a day earlier than the Judeans. Maybe Passover was always celebrated for two days in the days of the Master, as is the case in the Diaspora nowadays. If so, the Jewish people kept two consecutive Seder nights. None of these theories, however, find any corroboration in rabbinic literature or Jewish history. They have no basis in reality, and they would never have been proposed if not for the attempt to solve the discrepancy.

Another theory claims that the Synoptic Gospels were not actually describing a Passover meal, but a special meal meant to prepare for Passover. The plain reading of the Gospels makes that reinterpretation impossible:

> *And on the first day of Unleavened Bread, when they sacrificed the Passover lamb, his disciples said to him, "Where will you have us go and prepare for you to eat the Passover?"*
> ~Mark 14:12

> *I will keep the Passover at your house with my disciples.*
> Matthew 26:18

> *I have earnestly desired to eat this Passover with you before I suffer.*
> ~Luke 22:15

In every one of these verses, please note, the word "Passover" refers specifically to the Passover sacrifice, the lamb itself, which could only be sacrificed on the fourteenth day of Nissan and could only be eaten that night as the Yom Tov of the fifteenth of Nisan began. According to these three gospels, Yeshua told his disciples to go to the Temple, sacrifice a lamb as a Passover sacrifice, roast it, and bring it to the upper room. Our Master and His disciples ate more than just bread and wine that night—they ate the meat of the Passover sacrifice.

Finally, one popular theory explains that Yeshua and his disciples adopted the Qumran community's solar calendar, which was apparently followed by the Essenes. That calendar works independent of the lunar calendar and places the Yom Tov of Passover on a Wednesday every year. According to the Essene calendar, the seder must occur on a Tuesday night. Those who advance this idea suggest that Yeshua and His disciples celebrated a Passover Seder in the home of an Essene, several days before the normal day of

Passover was celebrated by the rest of the Jewish people. Some go so far as to suggest that Yeshua himself was Essene.

Most scholars have completely rejected the plausibility of this explanation. It requires an interval of several days between the arrest in Gethsemane and the crucifixion, not at all indicated in the Gospels. It also requires us to suppose that Yeshua followed the Essene calendar, which is totally out of character with what we know of Yeshua and His followers.

Evidence for John's Chronology

Raymond Brown examines the internal evidence within the Gospels to see which account is most probable. He concludes that the chronology presented in the Gospel of John best fits the evidence. He finds several problems within the story in Matthew, Mark, and Luke, difficulties which make it difficult to accept that all these things happened on a Yom Tov, which Jewish people observed as a holiday sabbath. From a historical perspective, it is impossible to imagine first-century, religious Jews (even if they were Sadducees) carrying out a trial and condemnation and participating in a Roman court procedure on a Yom Tov. Not to mention Joseph of Arimathea purchasing supplies on a Yom Tov.

External evidence supports the Johanine version as well. The apocryphal Gospel of Peter tells the story of the trial and death of our Master. The Gospel of Peter never made the cut for the canonical New Testament. It appears to have been written in the late second century. A sizable portion of it was rediscovered in 1886. The Gospel of Peter has no real credibility as a historically reliable source, but it at least tells us how the passion narrative's chronology was understood in the second-century church. It records a conversation between Pilate and Herod Antipas which firmly places the Master's crucifixion on Passover Eve.

When [Joseph of Arimathaea] knew that they were about to crucify him, he came to Pilate and asked for the Lord's body for burial. Pilate sent word to Herod, asking for the body. Herod said, "Brother Pilate, even if no one had asked for him we would have buried him, since the Sabbath is dawning. For it is written in the Law that the sun must not set on one who has been killed." And he delivered him over to the people the day before their Feast of Unleavened Bread. (3–5)

According to this passage, the execution took place on an Erev Shabbat and on the eve of Passover, i.e. Friday afternoon of Nisan 14.

A second piece of external evidence comes from the Talmud, tractate Sanhedrin (43a), where it says, "On the eve of the Passover Yeshu was hanged … he was hanged on the eve of the Passover." One manuscript of the Talmud even says, "On Erev Shabbat and Erev Pesach Yeshua was hanged." The Talmud has no better claim to historical reliability than the Gospel of Peter, but it does tell us how the passion narrative's chronology was understood (and remembered) in the Jewish community.

If these sources are correct, and if the Gospel of John is correct, it seems that Yeshua could not have celebrated a Seder with His disciples the night before he died.

The Academic Answer

Raymond Brown and most scholars who have studied this issue advise letting go of the Synoptic Gospels' version of the story. In other words, Jesus could not have kept a Passover Seder with his disciples. The Synoptic Gospels are simply wrong.

For example, *Biblical Archaeology Review*, Bible History Daily for April 11, 2014, offers a thorough article on this very topic. The article, by Jonathan Klawans, is titled "Was Jesus' Last Supper a Seder?" Like Brown, Klawans looks at the evidence and concludes that we have to follow John's chronology because the Synoptic version just does not make sense. So the academic world is ready to throw out the Last Seder presented in Matthew, Mark, and Luke.

Lichtenstein's Answer

The academic solution does not work for us in Messianic Judaism. We cannot just throw out the testimony of three gospels. Fortunately, we do not need to dismiss the Synoptic version or John's version.

Rabbi Yechiel Tzvi Lichtenstein's nineteenth-century Hebrew commentary on the gospels proposes a harmonization which retains both the Synoptic version and the Johanine version without dealing violence to the text of either. His explanation is speculative, but he bases that speculation on solid Jewish sources to present how it could have happened (and apparently did happen at least once) that there were two days of Passover, back-to-back, perhaps in the year the Master died.

Lichtenstein's explanation, however, is highly technical and requires the reader to have a great deal of background knowledge about the Jewish calendar, how it works, how it is reckoned, and how the holidays fit onto the calendar. Frankly, his explanation is beyond the scope of most gospel readers. Those interested in studying it out in detail can find the full argument with all the supporting evidence in my own commentary on the Gospels, *Chronicles of the Messiah*.

Lichtenstein explains that in the days of the Master, the Pharisees and the Sadducees had a great debate about how to observe Passover. The debate centered around the Counting of the Omer, that is the day of the first fruits of barley that begins the forty-nine day count off to Shavuot. The Torah says that the priests should offer the first fruits of the barley "on the day after the Sabbath" at Passover, but the Torah does not specify what it means by "the day after the Sabbath" (Leviticus 23:11). Does that mean after the Yom Tov of Passover or the day after the weekly Sabbath that falls during the seven days of unleavened bread? The Pharisees said, "It means Nisan 16, the day after Yom Tov." The Sadducees said, "It means Sunday, the day after the weekly Sabbath (Shabbat Chol HaMo'ed)." The Pharisees always won these type of arguments because they had the strength of tradition behind them, and they had the popular opinion of the people, the masses, supporting them. Whenever the Sadducean priests tried to do things the Sadducean way, the people revolted. They insisted on the traditional way. They literally forced the Sadducees to comply with Pharisaic tradition.

In those days, the new Sanhedrin determined the new moon and the beginning of the month by observation. Witnesses who sighted the new moon reported it to the Sanhedrin, and the Sanhedrin declared that the month had begun.

Lichtenstein says that, in the year our Master died, Erev Pesach (Nissan 14) must have fallen on a Thursday. Lichtenstein believes that the Sadducees hired false witnesses to forestall the month by one day. They used bribes to influence the Sanhedrin to delay declaring the new moon by one day, therefore forcing Erev Pesach (Nisan 14) to fall on a Friday that year. This made the Yom Tov of Passover (Nisan 15) coincide with the weekly Sabbath.

Why did they do that? Because then they could keep their cake and eat it too. They were able to count the Omer and celebrate Shavu'ot the way they wanted because they had forced the festival Yom Tov and the weekly Sabbath to coincide, therefore fulfilling both the Pharisaic opinion and their own. In this way, they forced the whole population, just for that year, to keep Shavu'ot on the day they wanted. Naturally, some people rejected the ruse and kept Passover a day earlier, but the majority went along with the decision of the court.

What did our Master do? Lichtenstein speculates that, because Yeshua knew He would not be able to keep the Seder with His disciples on Friday night, He took advantage of the fact that some belligerent Pharisees were keeping Passover a day early, according to their own reckoning of the month. Yeshua went to the home of someone who was doing that so that He could eat the Passover sacrifice with His disciples a day before the rest of the nation did and before He suffered:

"I have earnestly desired to eat this Passover with you before I suffer."

~Luke 22:15

Lichtenstein points out that this is not permissible ordinary circumstances. Ordinarily one should follow the majority and the ordained authorities that determine the Jewish calendar. Yeshua and His disciples followed the majority calendar and the authority of the Sanhedrin on other holy days. On this occasion, however, He had no other way to keep a final seder with His disciples. He joined the Pharisaic schism which was holding their seder a day before the day that had been declared by the Sadducees. The calendar problem that year made it permissible for Him to do so because many people in Israel were doing so also.

Lichtenstein writes:

Yeshua did this rightly, for by the principles of the Pharisees, both of these days were valid as holy days, because the sanctification of the pilgrim feasts depended upon the court and upon the people of Israel; for it is Israel that sanctifies the times. Even if they err or act presumptuously, the day is still holy—as I suggest above—and Yeshua's disciples understood this. It was only because his hour was near and he wanted to fulfill the commandment of the Passover that he joined himself with this sect, to eat his Passover on the fifth day in the evening. And if not this, he would have waited until the next day in line with the majority of Israel. That is why, I believe, his disciples imagined that he was asking Judas to buy things needed for the Feast, as it appears to me in John 13:29. For the main feast was the next day in the evening for the majority of Israel. Understand this.

It appears that divine Providence foresaw that in the year of Yeshua's death, it would occur like this in Israel, so that the Master would eat the Passover with his disciples and would fix a "meal on the holy evening," and along with this would be killed on the eve of Passover, thus himself becoming the true

*Passover lamb, as Paul writes in 1 Corinthians 5:7, and John
in his Gospel at 19:36 (q.v.).*

~Lichtenstein
Commentary on the New Testament, on Matthew 26:18

Lichtenstein finds support for this theory from the Talmud which
describes how, on one occasion, the Sadducees bribed witnesses
to manipulate the date of Passover. Lichtenstein says that this is
further explained in the Rashi and Tosafot on the passage, and if
you are interested, you can study the argument further in *Chronicles
of the Messiah.*

Conclusion

Thanks to the machinations of the Sadducean-controlled Sanhedrin, the people of Israel were divided that year. Most people were
keeping the calendar according to the ruling of the Sanhedrin as
the Torah instructs, but some Pharisees refused. They kept Passover
according to their own lunar reckoning. The Synoptic Gospels
report the minority, sectarian, Pharisaic chronology for Passover
that year whereas John reports the accepted majority reckoning
endorsed by the (Sadducean) Sanhedrin.

Lichtenstein's explanation is not bullet-proof, but it's the most
reasonable explanation I have heard so far, and I think I've heard
them all. It's the only one that has support from both rabbinic
literature and all four Gospels. Rabbi Lichtenstein's explanation
has the advantage of bringing Matthew, Mark, Luke, and John
together. We do not have to throw out either testimony. It allows
us to accept that Yeshua did keep a last Passover Seder with His
disciples, and He did suffer and die on Passover at the time of
the Passover sacrifice, only a few hours before the majority of the
people of Israel celebrated their seder that year.

This has implications for the Messianic Jewish observance of
Passover. We should keep the Seder in remembrance of the Master
as He instructed us to do. We should do so on the conventional

seder night along with the rest of the Jewish people, but we should keep in mind that, in the year He died, our Master kept his Last Seder one night earlier than most people did. This was an exception, not His normal mode of operation.

Does it matter? I think it does. It matters because the integrity and reliability of the Gospel testimony is at stake. It matters because our Master told us, "Do this in remembrance of me."

"I have been impressed with the urgency of doing. Knowing is not enough; we must apply. Being willing is not enough; we must do."

~Leonardo da Vinci

Last Seder
A Jewish Reading of the Last Supper
by D. T. Lancaster

On the night before he suffered, Jesus ate a "last supper" with his disciples. At that meal, He gave them bread and wine and told them to take the bread and wine in remembrance of Him. Thanks to increasing levels of education in the Jewish roots of Christianity, most Christians today realize that the Last Supper of Jesus and His disciples was a traditional Jewish Passover Seder meal, but most Christians probably still do not realize exactly how the Last Supper conforms to a traditional seder meal. The following article is based on *Torah Club Volume Four: Chronicles of the Messiah*, a commentary on the Gospels from a Messianic Jewish perspective.

The Typical Passover Seder

Although the various elements of the traditional Passover Seder have undergone alterations and development over the centuries, today's seder meal liturgy resembles the one conducted by Jesus and his disciples in the upper room. The Hebrew word seder means "set order," and the set order of conducting a Passover meal seems to have been established early. Jewish writings describe the set order of the Passover meal as it was practiced in the days of Jesus and the disciples.

In those days, the seder meal began after dark. No one ate any-thing from midday until they had all settled in around the table that night. Over the course of the evening, each person drank four ceremonial cups of wine. The first cup of wine accompa-nied a declaration of the day's holiness (kiddush). After the first cup, the ceremony commenced with bitter herbs and vegetables dipped into a vinegar sop (karpas). Then the servers put out the unleavened bread (matzah), fruit compote (charoset), and the Passover lamb. A child at the table asked the prescribed ques-tions. The father or host of the seder replied with an exposition of Deuteronomy 26:5–9 and a discussion of the significance of the ritual foods: the Passover sacrifice, the unleavened bread, and the bitter herbs. The recitation of Psalms 113–114 (Hallel) and a blessing in thanks of redemption preceded the second cup and the meal. After the meal, they poured a third cup to accompany the grace after meals, and the fourth and final cup accompanied the conclusion of the seder and as they sang the remainder of the psalms of Hallel (Psalms 115–118).

Around the Master's Table

> *They went and found it like he said to them, and they pre-pared the pesach. When the hour arrived, he reclined with the twelve apostles.*
> ~Lukas 22:14, Delitzsch Hebrew English

Simon Peter and John saw to the preparations: wine, unleavened bread, bitter herbs, vinegar for dipping, fruit compote, and the roasted sacrificial lamb. Cushions and mats surrounded the low, horseshoe shaped triklinium table. The table accommodated as many as thirteen participants. About five people could sit on the left and five on the right with the remaining ones reclining at the narrower center table. Everyone reclined along the outside of the table, allowing the inside of the table to remain accessible to the servers. Even to this day, participants in a Passover Seder lean to one side when eating the ceremonial foods as a remembrance of those days when everyone reclined around the seder table.

Foretaste of What is to Come

Before even taking the first of the four cups, He declared,

> *"I have deeply longed to eat this pesach with you before my suffering. For I say to you, I will not eat it again until it is fulfilled in the kingdom of God."*
> ~Lukas 22:15–16 DHE

He anticipated a period of separation from His disciples, but He also foresaw the day when He would be reunited with them to celebrate the grand seder at the Messianic banquet in the kingdom of heaven, i.e., the Messianic Era.

Judaism teaches that, at the Messianic banquet in the kingdom, the Messiah will receive His coronation rites, take four cups in His hands, and pronounce the blessings over wine preserved in its grapes since the foundation of the world. The twelve disciples came to Jerusalem expecting just such a festive meal. They anticipated a violent upheaval, throwing off the Roman yoke, followed by the coronation of the king. They had expected a resurrection of the dead and a great banquet with the Messiah. Instead, they had a simple seder with the Master, a foretaste of the appointed time to come.

The First of Four Cups

> *Participants in a Passover Seder drink four cups of wine. This rule goes back to the days of Jesus. The rabbis said, "A person must have not less than four cups of wine at Passover, even if they must be paid for from the funds devoted to charity for the poor."*
> ~Mishnah

The Gospel of Luke specifically mentions two cups at the Last Supper. Matthew and Mark mention only one cup, but we can assume that Jesus and His disciples did take all four cups. In Jewish tradition, all four cups are considered one cup, called "The Cup of Salvations."

Luke says, "He took the cup and made a [blessing] and said 'Take it and distribute it.'" (Lukas 22:17 DHE). The blessing over wine was simply, "Blessed are you, LORD our God, King of the universe who creates the fruit of the vine." Jesus may have added a second blessing pertaining to the festival day, making mention of the Exodus from Egypt and the sanctity of the festival season. Then He took a solemn vow, vowing to abstain from wine and the Pesach meal until He is able to drink and eat with His disciples again in the Messianic Era:

> *For I say to you, I will surely not drink the fruit of the vine from now until the kingdom of God comes.*
> ~Lukas 22:17 DHE

This does not mean that He abstained from the cup that night at the table. Jewish law requires that one who makes a blessing over food or drink must taste of the thing for which he has blessed God. Jesus drank from the first cup and passed it to His disciples.

Karpas and the Traitor

After the first cup, participants in the Passover Seder wash hands and then take part in a ritual called karpas. The ritual involves dipping a green vegetable twice into red wine vinegar. (In modern seders, salt water often substitutes for the wine vinegar.) The meaning of the ritual is obscure, but according to some opinions, it represents the betrayal of Joseph whose brothers dipped his coat in goat's blood—the event that initiated the descent into Egypt. It may also represent dipping the hyssop into the lamb's blood.

As the Master and his disciples dipped the karpas into the dish of vinegar, he said, "Amen, I say you, one of you will betray me."

~Mattai 26:21 DHE

He further said, "Look—the hand of the one betraying me is with me on the table."

~Lukas 22:21 DHE

The disciples reacted with shock. They were greatly grieved and each man began to say to Him, "Is it I my master?" Jesus replied with an allusion to the karpas ritual. He answered and said,

"The man who dipped his hand in the bowl with me is the one who will betray me."

~Mattai 26:23 DHE

The other disciples had not observed whose hand dipped into the vinegar simultaneously with the Master, but Judas Iscariot knew.

Gospel readers unfamiliar with the seder might assume that the dipping into the bowl with Iscariot (reported in Matthew and Mark) is the same as John 13:26 where Jesus dips a piece of bread and hands it to Iscariot, but the two incidents refer to different rituals during the course of the seder.

Iscariot alone knew that his hand had dipped the karpas into the vinegar at the same moment as the hand of Jesus. This indicates that Iscariot must have been reclining next to Jesus at the table. Carrying on the pretense of ignorance, Iscariot turned to the Master and asked, along with the others, "Rabbi, is it I?" He said to him privately, "You have said it."

The Matzah in Remembrance

The meal continued. An ancient Jewish description of the seder

*meal says, "Next they bring unleavened bread, lettuce, and fruit
compote (charoset) ... in the days of the Temple they would set
before him the body of the Passover lamb."*

~Mishnah

Before eating the lamb, the participants at a seder had to dis-
charge their obligation to eat unleavened bread (matzah) and bitter
herbs. For the duration of the festival, no grain product exposed
to moisture (and allowed to rise before baking) can be eaten or
brought into the home. The Torah commands the Jewish people
to eat unleavened matzah-bread on each of the seven days of the
festival and specifically during the seder.

During the course of the seder meal, the master of the table lifts
the unleavened bread and declares, "This is the bread of affliction."
Later, he says the blessing for bread, breaks it, and distributes it to
everyone at the table.

Jesus made the blessing for bread: "Blessed are you, LORD our
God, king of the universe, who brings forth bread from the earth."
He may have added the additional blessing for the festival, "... who
has sanctified us with his commandments and has commanded us
about eating *matzah.*" Then He broke the bread of affliction, ate
some, and distributed it among His disciples, telling them, "Take,
eat; this is my body which is given for you; do this in remembrance
of me."

He instructed His disciples to henceforth eat the unleavened
bread of Passover in remembrance of Him. With those words,
He invested the Passover ritual with new, additional significance.
Previously, the disciples of Jesus ate the unleavened bread at
Passover in remembrance of the Exodus from Egypt. The Torah
explicitly says that Passover "will be a memorial (*zikkaron*) to
you" (Exodus 12:14).

Christian tradition has embellished the ritual, but the original
context indicates a simple, Passover rite common to every Jewish
home, albeit, augmented with additional symbolic associations.

By declaring the unleavened bread as a symbol for His body, the Master invited the disciples to henceforth remember Passover as the occasion of His suffering and sacrifice. As Paul says,

> *"For as often as you eat this bread ... you proclaim the Lord's death until he comes."*
> ~1 Corinthians 11:26

Korech

Our Master Jesus distributed the unleavened *matzah*-bread according to seder custom and turned His attention to the bitter herbs and Passover lamb. After a blessing for the bitter herbs and the lamb, they began to eat the main course.

As they ate, Jesus became troubled in spirit, and He testified and said,

> *"Amen, amen, I say to you that one of you will betray Me."*
> ~Yochanan 13:21 DHE

Again the disciples began looking at one another, at a loss to know of which one He spoke. The twelve men had spent the last three years together in the most incredible of adventures. They had walked and talked, learned and argued, eaten and drank, camped and traveled together. They had seen the sea calmed, the sick healed, demons cast out, and the dead raised. Their shared experiences forged a bond of fraternity out of which betrayal must have seemed unimaginable. The unspeakable thought broke their hearts.

John the son of Zebedee reclined at the table beside the Master. Iscariot may have reclined in the place of honor on the Master's left. That arrangement explains how Iscariot dipped into the dish (*karpas*) at the same time as the Master and how Jesus could easily give him the morsel.

Simon Peter nodded from across the table to get John's attention.

He said to him confidentially, "Tell us who it is of whom he is speaking." John leaned back and asked in a whisper, "Master, who is it?"

Jesus replied softly, "That is the one for whom I shall dip the morsel and give it to him." Jesus dipped the morsel into a dish, and he handed it to Iscariot:

> *Yeshua answered, "Watch—it is the one to whom I dip my piece and give it." He dipped his piece and gave it to Yehudah ben Shim'on Ish-Keriyot. After he swallowed it, the satan came within him. Yeshua said to him, "What you will do, do quickly."*
>
> ~Yochanan 13:26–27 DHE

This ritual is called "*korech.*" According to the custom, one should combine the matzah-bread, the Passover lamb, and the bitter herbs, and eat them together (korech) as a sort of sandwich to literally fulfill the verse that says,

> *"They shall eat it with unleavened bread and bitter herbs."*
>
> ~Numbers 9:11

The bitter herbs remind the participants in a seder of the bitterness of the suffering in Egypt. For disciples of the Master, the bitter herbs also remind them of the bitterness of the night He was betrayed and of the onset of His suffering.

In seders today, we have no Passover lamb, but we still perform korech by dipping unleavened bread into fruit compote (charoset) and bitter herbs (maror), such as grated horseradish root. The volcanic effect of horseradish on matzah allows one to experience the culinary equivalent of John's statement regarding Judas,

> *"After he swallowed it, the satan came within him."*
>
> ~Yochanan 13:27 DHE

The Third Cup

He said to them, "This is my blood, the blood of the new covenant, which is poured out on behalf of many."
~Markos 14:23 DHE

After eating the Passover meal, participants in a Passover Seder pour a third cup of wine to accompany grace after meals. Some refer to the third cup as the cup of thanksgiving because it accompanies the prayer of thanks for the food. Likewise, Paul refers to the cup of the Master as "the cup of thanksgiving." (1 Corinthians 10:16)

The text in Luke and 1 Corinthians explicitly states that Jesus took the cup "after they had eaten," "after the meal." That can only be the third cup, the cup of thanksgiving. The Greek word *eucharisteo* means "to give thanks" and, in this context, implies only the traditional Jewish practice of pronouncing a blessing to accompany a meal. The sacramental meaning of the word "Eucharist" developed in later Christian tradition.

Our Master said the blessing for wine and distributed the cup to His disciples, saying, "Drink from it, all of you; for this cup is the new covenant in My blood, which is poured out for many for the forgiveness of sins. Do this, as often as you drink it, in remembrance of Me."

As He passed the cup of thanksgiving to His disciples, Jesus instructed them to henceforth take the wine of Passover in remembrance of Him. With those words, He once again invested new symbolism into the Passover ceremony. He did not institute a new ritual or replace the previous symbolic associations. Previously, the disciples of Jesus drank four cups at Passover in remembrance of the salvation from Egypt. As stated above, God ordained Passover as a "memorial" of the exodus. Rabbi Jesus told His disciples to henceforth take the cups of Passover in remembrance of Him.

Again, Christian tradition has embellished the ritual of the cup, but the original context indicates a simple, Passover rite common to every Jewish home, albeit augmented with additional symbolic associations. The ritual cup of the Master symbolizes His willing, sacrificial death:

> *"For as often as you ... drink the cup, you proclaim the Lord's death until he comes."*
>
> ~1 Corinthians 11:26

As noted above, the traditional blessing for wine thanks God for creating the fruit of the vine. As He passed the cup to His disciples, Jesus said,

> *"Amen. I say to you, I will surely not drink of the fruit of the vine again until that day when I will drink it new in the kingdom of God."*
>
> ~Markos 14:25 DHE

What does He mean when he says that He will drink the wine "new" with His disciples? Jewish tradition explains that, when the Messiah comes, He will host a great banquet in the kingdom, and He will serve wine that has been preserved since the creation of the world.

Fourth Cup and Singing the Hallel

> *After their recital of the Hallel ...*
>
> ~Mattai 26:30 DHE

In the days of the Master, participants in a Passover Seder sang through the Hallel (Psalms 113–118). They recited a portion of the psalms before the food in conjunction with the second cup, and they recited the remainder of the psalms after the meal in conjunction with the final cup. The Gospels mention Jesus and the disciples keeping the same custom:

"And when they had sung a hymn, they went out to the Mount of Olives."
                                    ~Matthew 26:30; Mark 14:26

Before they left for the Mount of Olives, however, they lingered over the fourth cup.

Jesus said the blessing for the last cup. In conjunction with the last blessings over the fruit of the vine, He said,

"I am the vine and you are the branches.
                                    ~John 15:5

They talked at the table long into the night as the Master delivered his farewell discourse to His disciples. He spoke all the sayings recorded in John 13–17. He warned the disciples that they would deny Him. Simon Peter adamantly insisted he would never betray Jesus. He told them to prepare for the trauma to come, and He prayed for them.

When Jesus finished His farewell discourse, He left the table. His disciples followed him. They went out from the city, crossed the valley at the foot of the Mount of Olives, and climbed the hill to the garden of Gethsemane. Then Jesus prayed,

"My Father, if only you were willing to make this cup pass from me! Yet let it not be according to my will but according to your will."
                                    ~Lukas 22:42 DHE

"The greatest deception men suffer is from their own opinions."
~Leonardo da Vinci

ACKNOWLEDGEMENTS

Sybil E. Jarrells is the muse that has created my writing. She encourages, refuses to read my writing until it is published, and is the epitome of the support behind the man. She is my gift from God.

Others are certainly important. Mike Parker, publisher, has shown interest, support, and confidence in the results of my writing and I am honored to call him friend. Judy Powell, Lynn Pearson McClendon, and Harriette Edmonds are the intellect behind the scenes. They fulfill the most important role as editors. They make me look smart.

I can not let these acknowledgements end without recognizing the trio religious educators who have read and commented on the manuscript; Rev. Dr. John Lanny Lanford, Rev. Dr. Kaye Dalton and Rev. Dr. David Dalton.

This book is also dedicated to you, readers. Without readers, an author's work is the essence of the quote from Shakespeare's *Hamlet*—"sound and fury, signifying nothing."

Daniel Thomas Lancaster is the Educational Director at First Fruits of Zion (ffoz.org) and Pastor of Beth Immanuel Sabbath Fellowship (bethimmanuel.org)in Hudson Wisconsin. Lancaster is the author of *Torah Club*, (torahclub.org) a messianic commentary series from First Fruits of Zion and has authored more than a few books on messianic apologetics including *Grafted*

In, The Holy Epistle to the Galatians, Restoration, and *Elementary Principles.* See a video by Daniel at https://www.facebook.com/watch/?v=10154164237060006.

"Hosting a Seder" by D. T. Lancaster reprinted by permission of the author.

"Last Supper or Last Seder?" by D. T. Lancaster reprinted by permission of the author.

"Last Seder: A Jewish Reading of the Last Supper" by D. T. Lancaster reprinted by permission of the author.

Last but certainly not least I offer this acknowledgement of Jesus the Christ without whom there would be no Last Supper and no redemption from our sins.

SOURCES

www.artincontext.org
www.wikipedia.com
www.biblegateway
www.leonardodavinci.net
www.britannica.com
www.contexttravel.com
www.mentalfloss.com
www.unmuseum.org
www.greekreporter.com
www.nocodyslexia.com
www.spellzone.com

Where the spirit does not work with the hand, there is no art.
~Leonardo da Vinci

About the Author

Ralph E. Jarrells entered the field of writing novels late in his life. He retired from corporate America a decade ago and began an award winning video production company that specialized in creating video programs for ministry and mission organizations. So far, his work has received 18 international creative awards.

He retired from a successful career in marketing, advertising and publishing that included senior executive positions with major corporations—Sr. VP Marketing with an international franchise company, VP Marketing with a NYSE company, VP Account Supervisor for the world's largest advertising company and Editorial director for a major trade magazine publishing company.

Connect with Ralph online at:

www.ralphejarrellsauthor.com

Also Available From

WordCrafts Press

Ponderings: Thoughts on Consecration, Discipleship, Worship & Presence
by Wayne Berry

Elders at the Gate: A Call to Repair the Generational Links
by Ray Blunt

Donkey Tales: Exploring Perspectives from the Bible's Stubborn Creatures
by Keith Alexis

A Pastor's Secrets: For Young Pastors and those wanting to be a Pastor
by Ronnie Meek

Deconstructing a Disciple's Doubt
by Dr. Jason Lee McKinney